IN THE WAKE OF THE PORTUGUESE NAVIGATORS

A photographic essay by

MICHAEL TEAGUE

CARCANET

in association with the

CALOUSTE GULBENKIAN FOUNDATION

Dedicated to the memory of
Avelino Teixeira da Mota (1920-1982)

First published in Great Britain in 1988

Photographs © Michael Teague 1988
Text © Michael Teague 1988
Designed by *José Brandão*
Colour separations: Secor/Macau
Photographic prints: Fotocolor, Lisbon

Printed and bound in Portugal by Printer Portuguesa for
Carcanet Press Limited
208-212 Corn Exchange Buildings
Manchester M4 3BQ
and (Portuguese edition)
Quetzal Editores
Rua Sanches Coelho, n.º 3, 9, Esq.
1600 Lisboa

This book is the first in a series *Aspects of Portugal* to be published in Great Britain by Carcanet Press in association with the Calouste Gulbenkian Foundation and with collaboration from the Anglo-Portuguese Foundation.

SERIES EDITORS: *Eugénio Lisboa, Michael Schmidt, Kim Taylor*

British Library Cataloguing in Publication Data
Teague, Michael
In the wake of the Portuguese navigators
I. Title
910'.9469

ISBN 0 85635 823 1 (cased)
ISBN 0 85635 824 X (paper)

Acknowledgements

I would like to thank the Calouste Gulbenkian Foundation in Lisbon for sponsoring some of my early travels in Asia and especially the Department for Cooperation with the New African States for its promotion of a travelling exhibition and for acquiring a number of my pictures for the Foundation's permanent collection.

The Secretaria de Estado da Cultura was also most helpful in organising an exhibition, which circulated in many parts of the world. I am particularly grateful to Lourdes Simões de Carvalho for her careful orchestration of this project. Without her support and encouragement, I doubt whether this book would ever have been completed.

My thanks also go to Kim Taylor who, as the director of the Calouste Gulbenkian Foundation (U. K. Branch), was active in his support of the English version of this book as part of a series on Portuguese themes. To Maria da Piedade Ferreira of Quetzal Editores and Michael Schmidt of Carcanet Press my gratitude for their patience and forbearance in coordinating the many details of the English and Portuguese editions.

I would also like to thank José Brandão and his wife Salette for all the care they took with every aspect of the design and layout.

Finally, I would like to express my warmest gratitude and appreciation to all those who over the years helped me to develop my interest in Portugal and who assisted, in one way or another, in this photographic odyssey which took me around the world.

From the bleak, rocky promontory at Sagres,
Prince Henry the Navigator
directed the first epic voyages of discovery
in search of the sea-route to the Indies.

Sea of Portugal

O bitter sea, how much of all your gall
Is bitter tears of Portugal!
That we crossed you, how many mothers wept,
How many sons vain vigil kept!
How many maids betrothed remain unwed
That you, sea, might be ours instead!

Was it worth while? Anything is, if
A soul of man is great enough.
He who would round the cape must not give up
But in its Storms see his Good Hope.
Danger and depth God to the sea has given
But in it he has mirrored heaven.

FERNANDO PESSOA
(from *Mensagem*)
translated from the Portuguese
by Keith Bosley

Azores

Lisbon
Sagres
Ceuta
Madeira
Arzila
Mazagan

Ormuz
Bahrain
Diu
Muscat
Daman
Bassein
Goa
Madras
Calicut
Cochin
Galle

Nagasaki

Macau

Ayutthaya

Cape Verde
Cacheu

Gondar
Aden

Elmina

Malacca

Belém

Príncipe
S. Tomé

Recife

Rio Congo
Luanda
Muxima

Malindi
Mombasa
Zanzibar

Timor

Diamantina

Tete

Ouro Preto
Salvador (Bahia)

Mozambique Island

Rio de Janeiro

Sofala

Cape of Good Hope

Atlantic Ocean

Indian Ocean

Author's Route

My interest in Portugal and the Portuguese world began over thirty years ago. I was a student at Oxford and won the annual university essay prize offered by the Royal Asian Society. The subject that year was 'The Rise and Fall of Portuguese Colonial Activities East of Suez'. Why Suez, I wondered, imagining a phantom Tordesillas line drawn in the east as well as the west. By relying heavily on the erudite, wide-ranging and lively works of Charles Boxer, then as now my *guru* on the subject, I produced my 5,000 word piece, the only one, I suspect, which was submitted that year.

The President of the Society, awarding me the prize, drew attention to the fact that I was born in India where my first *ayah* (nurse) had come from Goa. 'Don't let us underestimate the influence of the cradle', he said, and handed me a small but very welcome cheque and a large certificate recording the fact that the prize had been 'founded in 1901 by the generosity of His Highness the Raja of Cochin, the Maharaja Gajapati Rao, the Raja of Parlakimedi and other Chiefs and Gentlemen of Southern India.'

The following year I was invited on a university expedition to Angola. There were four of us in the group: a botanist, a geologist, a zoologist and myself, a student of history. We knew very little about where we were going, although for months beforehand we had pored over old tomes with titles such as *Across Angola With My Wife*. There was little about the country written in English and at that stage we knew no Portuguese, although we struggled with countless linguaphone records, which seemed obsessively concerned with the intricacies of the household arrangements of 'a família Magalhães'.

Angola seemed a distant, exotic place closed especially to foreigners, and it exerted more and more of an attraction as the time for our departure approached. But with travel to remoter, wilder shores, one's expectations are often far from the mark. I don't know exactly what I expected of Angola but nothing prepared me for the sheer beauty of the place, its vast scale and scenic variety and the diversity of its people.

We spent our first few weeks in the south-western corner of the country, high on the Huila Plateau. The countryside was heavily cultivated in parts, completely wild and untamed in others. It was my first experience of the 'big sky' of Africa, where large herds of game — unparked and unreserved so to speak — galloped toward distant horizons and one could spend days without seeing any sign of human life. The scientists were ecstatic with their exotic finds, but after several weeks of life in the wild, I hankered to go north to the capital, Luanda, where I had heard there were some fine examples of historical architecture. Like everything else in Angola, this, too, exceeded my expectations.

In a continent which has a tendency to swallow up traces of the past almost as fast as they are planted, it was a delight to find that Luanda was unique not only in the beauty of its setting but in the wealth of its historical interest. Founded in 1575 by the grandson of Bartolomeu Dias, it was the first European settlement in West Africa which was built as a city on the traditional Portuguese pattern of an upper and lower town connected by narrow, winding streets known as *ladeiras*. Quite a number of old buildings still stood, including several extremely fine seventeenth century churches, a rare sight in Africa. They were simple, unpretentious constructions which relied for effect on the beauty of their proportions rather than on wealth of detail and ornamentation. They were poor cousins of their counterparts in Brazil and, in simpler vein, reflected some of the architectural style of eighteenth century Bahia and Rio de Janeiro.

I was fascinated to see how, despite poor building materials and without skilled craftsmen, even the humblest of the old houses had been built with imaginative concessions to tropical living: windows carefully aligned for maximum cross-ventilation, roofs insulated against the heat with bamboo strips, wide verandahs and thick walls — all elements we tend to accept as elementary in tropical architecture, but which the Portuguese were pioneers in devising, not only in Africa and Brazil but in India and the Far East as well.

When I re-read the diaries I made on that first trip to Angola, I am intrigued to see how fascinated I was by my first exposure to Portuguese historical architecture and to that distinctive yet elusive quality of Portuguese style, to which I shall return. I wandered around the streets and alleys of Luanda for days photographing and taking notes. Some of these read like entries in the journal of a bird watcher in search of elusive species. 'Saw a large pink and white *casa nobre* today with ferns on the balcony and a parrot perched on the railings', reads one entry. Another tells of 'a beautiful pale green and white town house on the Rua das Flores with many elegantly spaced windows and a beautifully proportioned *sobradinho*'. Elsewhere a note records: 'A small *casa típica* painted mustard yellow and maroon and shaded by royal palms beneath the pale pink fortress of São Miguel, which dates from the original founding of the city.'

And so the catalogue continues. I photographed what I could, but as I was on a limited budget and had to conserve film, I soon became adept at developing a selective eye. I am glad I recorded what I did because with the enormous growth of the city many of those old buildings have disappeared.

For me Luanda was new, unusual, different. I spent many evenings on the narrow island which guards the harbour and just enjoyed the view across the bay with the panorama of the city glowing in the evening light, the houses climbing gently over the hills, layer on layer in the fashion of many Portuguese towns, Lisbon in particular.

Until the middle of the nineteenth century Portugal had few settlements in the interior of Angola. There were consequently few plantations of any size and no tradition of country house architecture as in Brazil but a few fortified settlements were maintained up the River Kwanza, at places such as Muxima (1597), Massangano (1583) and Cambambe (1604). It was here that the Portuguese held out for over seven years when the Dutch seized Luanda in the seventeenth century. I visited these outposts which are superbly located above the gently-flowing river and found simple, sturdy constructions consisting of rather cramped little forts and heavily-buttressed, barn-like churches empty except for the wheeling of innumerable bats.

Angola was the apprenticeship of my Portuguese peregrinations. The following year I obtained a scholarship to study in Lisbon, and thus began my introduction to Portugal itself. It was a lovely summer, spent half among archives and half enjoying the pleasures and surprises of the country. Portugal has always promised the charm of the sudden view for me. You think you are on familiar ground, your eye gets conditioned to a certain set of architectural styles and principles and then suddenly you are brought up short by the unexpected. You can trace this pattern of contrasts from the rich background of the north, which seems to lend itself to the Baroque, to the rolling open country of the Alentejo, where simpler architectural forms are evident and on down to the Algarve in the south, which remains essentially Moorish in inspiration. For a tiny country the variations in style are enormous and it is fascinating to see how the Portuguese took them and improvised on them in so many parts of the world. It was my interest in these phenomena, nurtured in Angola and further fostered in Portugal, which drew me next, inevitably, to Brazil.

I ended up living there for almost three years, teaching English in Rio. They were a curious mixture of laziness and stimulation. In that pervasive, lotus-eating atmosphere, my quest for historical architecture became more a hobby than a dedicated search, although many corners of the city still retained attractive vestiges of the past: a Baroque church sandwiched between skyscrapers, the very narrow streets right in the centre of the city, some lovely old houses in hidden corners like the Largo do Boticário, the large waterfront square, pale replica of the magnificent Terreiro do Paço in Lisbon. The beauty of the city lay more in its extraordinary topography. I often used to go up to the top of Corcovado to watch the dawn come up because then you could get an idea of what the place might have looked like when the first settlers arrived. Unlike the Spaniards, the Portuguese never imposed the ubiquitous gridiron pattern on their cities overseas. Instead they grew, as someone said, 'like crabs crawling along the sea shore'.

Teaching allowed me long vacations and I made the most of them. The old mining towns of Minas Gerais became my favourite hunting ground for the Baroque, with Ouro Preto as the obvious first choice and Diamantina, less well known, a close second.

Almost hidden in a valley, Ouro Preto clings to the side of a mountain range, cascading and breaking into smaller settlements on the different hills which constitute the town. In many ways it epitomises the Golden Age of Brazil. It was an immensely wealthy city in the eighteenth century and this is reflected in the opulent elegance of its architecture. It has remained largely untouched, a museum town but still very much alive. I spent an Easter there. The days (and nights) were filled with processions and bands and services in the numerous churches, most of which seem to be perched on the tops of hills, so that we were constantly climbing and descending in apparently endless procession.

The churches of Ouro Preto follow a distinctive pattern reminiscent of those of the same period in northern Portugal. They have similar curved pediments, portly tower tops and simple façades with all the decoration centred around the doorways and windows. In Minas this decoration was usually carved out of the soft local soapstone, which allowed for a profusion of elements and a wealth of detail, standing out in bold relief against the brilliant whitewashed walls. In northern Portugal granite was used to give the same contrasting effect: in the Azores almost black basalt was employed, with even more dramatic results.

The soapstone carvings in Minas reached their apogee with the work of the celebrated mulatto sculptor Antonio Francisco Lisboa (1730-1814), nicknamed 'O Aleijadinho', whose work at Ouro Preto, São João Del-Rei, and most spectacularly of all at the pilgrimage church of Congonhas do Campo, are masterpieces of craftsmanship and creativity. The inspiration is Portuguese but the workmanship and the extraordinary wealth of detail are essentially Brazilian.

These examples of adaptation and improvisation on a basic theme increasingly occupied my interest. The Luso-Brazilian Baroque of the Minas churches and Aleijadinho's exquisite soapstone carvings are but one manifestation of this cultural cross-patterning. There were many others, both major and minor. I remember the owner of an old house in Ouro Preto showing me how the plaster on the walls had been laid down over a framework of plaited wicker. 'They don't make them like this anymore. The idea came from Africa', he told me. I knew. I had seen the same process used in the eighteenth century houses of Luanda. I found these connections and linkages fascinating. One can trace them in many other parts of the country.

In the old diamond-mining town of Diamantina, for instance, the predominant influence is Rococo rather than Baroque and the small town has a sparkling assortment of brilliantly painted houses with exotic curved roofs and a number of vaguely Tyrolean looking churches decorated in what can only be described as Brazilian Chinoiserie. The whole effect is bizarre and stimulating.

The early coastal settlements in north-eastern Brazil are very different in style from those of Minas. Salvador da Bahia is the finest example and was the first capital of the Portuguese colony. It still retains a quality like no other city in the country, an exhilarating mixture of Portugal, Africa and a lot else besides. It is the prototype of the Brazilian Lisbon and was in fact the first European city to be built in South America, just as Luanda was the first in West Africa. They share many of the same characteristics: a magnificent setting with an upper and a lower town, numerous hills, narrow winding streets, a superb bay and some exquisite old architecture.

Bahia reflects the wealth and importance of the early colony. Its elegant, sometimes ornate churches are full of *talha dourada,* the carved and gilded wooden decoration typical of the Portuguese Baroque of the period. Some of it, in the church of São Francisco de Assis for example, can become slightly over-wrought but never overwhelming. Unlike equivalent work in Spanish America, Portuguese *talha,* however intricate, seems to avoid going overboard by incorporating quieter, cooler elements, such as dadoes of blue and white *azulejos* (tiles), which serve the eye as a pleasant, relaxing contrast to the surrounding swirling gilt and gamboling cherubs.

Recife and Olinda to the north are less dramatic than Salvador da Bahia but very attractive nonetheless. The influence of the Dutch occupation of Pernambuco (1621-1654) is still evident there. The land is flatter, waterways and canals more prominent. In Pernambuco one is constantly reminded of the lovely landscapes of Franz Post, who spent several years there during the Dutch occupation. He left a series of paintings which more than any others seem to capture the essence of seventeenth century Brazil. I went in search of the perfect 'Post' *engenho* (sugar plantation) but never quite succeeded in finding one. They had become too industrialised. It is left to the imagination and to the evocative descriptions of Gilberto Freyre in *Casa Grande e Sanzala* to recreate that vanished world in the mind's eye. There always seemed to be a particular beauty about the self-contained world of the *engenhos* with their long, low single-storeyed buildings with wide verandahs and gently sloping roofs. The Portuguese rival the Chinese and Japanese in the variety, style and exquisite proportions of their roofs. This applies equally to the humblest and the grandest of constructions. It was in distinctive details such as these, as well as in the design of doorways, verandahs and balconies, the extraordinary range of colour contrasts between window frames and doors, and the subtle use of *azulejos,* a decorative feature the Portuguese have made uniquely their own, that I found my eye becoming increasingly attuned to the intricacies (and simplicities) of Portuguese style. Brazil was a rich training ground. After my stay there I was eager to press on further afield.

I conceived the idea of trying to recreate pictorially something of the atmosphere of the lands the Portuguese encountered on their way out to the East during the Age of the Discoveries, and of the architectural heritage they left in many parts of the world from Brazil to Japan.

It was an ambitious scheme and became something of a global treasure hunt as I followed my quarry from desert wastes to tropical jungle, from highland plateaux to lowland plains, up rivers and across seas. It soon became apparent to me that the wide and rich background variety of the old Portuguese world was quite extraordinary. It took me many months to complete the journey. Trains, buses, ships, planes, mules and even camels were used in search of things Portuguese. It is not a journey I could undertake today. When I made my trip I had plenty of time and little money — a combination which makes for interesting travel especially when one is young. Today many of the places I went to, such as the island of Ormuz at the mouth of the Persian Gulf, or Abyssinia and certain other parts of Africa and Asia, are either impossible to get to or extremely difficult of access. I'm glad I went when the going was good.

The journey I completed was essentially along the old sea-route to India from Lisboa to Goa with many, many stops along the way. Starting in Morocco, I travelled along the north African coast where the Portuguese had established a number of fortified settlements, beginning with the city of Ceuta, which they captured from the Moors in 1415. The magnificent fortifications they built there can still be seen today. Other Portuguese settlements such as Arzila near Tangier and Mazagan further down the coast also have some fine remains, especially Mazagan which remained a Portuguese possession until well into the eighteenth century. The casbah of the city is contained within the old fortifications, which front directly on to the sea. The white box-like houses appear totally encircled by the long tawny coloured walls. Set against the brilliant blue of sky and sea, and in the evening with the battlements silhouetted against the sunset, the effect is unforgettable. The underground water cisterns at Mazagan with their delicate fan-vaulted chambers are another reminder of the early Portuguese settlement and the main street of the town is still called Rua Direita although, as in most Portuguese towns, it runs anything but straight.

I wish I had spent more time in Morocco, especially in the far south, but I had to press on to the world of Senegambia and Guinea, areas long associated with the early exploration of West Africa. I was particularly interested in travelling up the Gambia River, which I did for over 350 miles in a battered river steamer in the best *African Queen* tradition. I knew the area well from the two years I had spend there doing my military service as an officer in the Gambia Regiment, which had the distinction of being the smallest regiment in the British Army, and I still retain a great affection for this tiny sliver of territory which has a special charm and distinctive flavour of its own.

Nearby in what is now Guinea-Bissau there are not many vestiges of early Portuguese settlement, with the exception of the small sixteenth century fort at Cacheu in the north, which appears almost toy-like in its Douanier Rousseau setting of mangrove-fringed river and dense clumps of palm. The country is ethnically diverse: over thirty different tribes live within its narrow frontiers. I relished the time I spent there as well as in the Cape Verde Islands, which lie some 500 miles out into the Atlantic. One could spend months exploring this fascinating archipelago of nine islands but I had to confine myself to the two main ones: São Vincente and São Tiago, where Praia, the capital, is located. A pleasant small town of dusty, pastel-shaded houses, Praia is set near the ruins of the older settlement of Cidade Velha, situated in a narrow valley, a wealth of ruined houses and churches tumbling down through groves of coconut palms to a sparkling sea.

Much further down the coast of the mainland the great castle of Elmina, built by the Portuguese in 1482, still stands as an imposing reminder of the past. Heavily rebuilt by the Dutch who captured it in the seventeenth century, it was the first and most spectacular of a number of commercial forts which the Portuguese built along the so-called Gold Coast. The others such as Axim and Shama pale beside the mediaeval splendour of Elmina with its huge bastions facing the sea and its elaborate inner courtyard.

After visiting the extraordinarily beautiful islands of São Tomé and Principe, which the Portuguese discovered in the Bight of Benin at the end of the fifteenth century and which are rich in historical and architectural interest, especially the self-contained world of the *roças* (cocoa plantations), I returned to Angola. This time I visited the old capital of the ancient Kingdom of Congo at São Salvador in the north. The Portuguese built a number of churches and established a mission there in the sixteenth century, converting the King and his court to Christianity. The ruins of the Jesuit mission can still be seen and a number of descendents of the old Congolese royal family were living there at that time, treasuring a motley collection of regalia that had been sent out as presents by the Kings of Portugal at various times. The story of the Kingdom of Congo is a fascinating but little known episode of African history.

While in northern Angola I travelled up the River Congo to the Yelala Rapids, some hundred miles from the mouth of the river. It was here that Diogo Cão, who discovered the river in 1482, left an inscription, which can still be clearly read today. How the tiny caravels of his fleet managed to get this far against the tremendous force of the current as it passes through the narrow gorge at Yelala is beyond comprehension. I nearly killed myself making the same trip in a powerful motor boat, hugging the shore most of the way.

It is extraordinary with what skill, courage and faith the Portuguese navigators set out on their voyages of discovery. The eighty years or so before Columbus crossed the Atlantic constitute a mediaeval space age saga. I had read about it in books, but not until I saw for myself the many places they ventured to against great odds did I fully realise what a remarkable feat these early exploratory voyages were.

As I continued around the southern tip of Africa, visiting the places connected with the rounding of the Cape of Good Hope by Bartolomeu Dias in 1487-88 and ascended the so-called 'wild coast' south of Durban where so many ships were wrecked, I became increasingly aware of just how rough and inhospitable much of this terrain must have appeared to the early navigators. It is hardly surprising that no attempt was made to settle there. Further up the coast in Mozambique the Portuguese established a number of settlements, the most important of which was on Mozambique Island in the north. It became the first capital of the colony. With its narrow streets, pastel coloured houses and churches, and guarded by the great fortress of São Sebastião, Mozambique Island remains one of the loveliest, most evocative places on the whole East African coast. It is so small and compact that one can easily walk from one end to the other, the brilliant blue of the coral sea visible everywhere. It naturally became a popular stopping-off place on the sea route to and from India. In fact a strong Indian influence remains there to this day, reflected particularly in the architectural style and decoration of many of the buildings.

The Portuguese presence in East Africa extended well beyond Mozambique; to Zanzibar, where the cloves which first attracted them to the island are still grown, their delicate aroma wafting miles out to sea; to Mombasa where they built Fort Jesus, an exceptionally fine fortress constructed in the shape of a cross, and further north to Malindi where Vasco da Gama picked up the Arab pilot who guided him on the last lap of his epic voyage to India in 1498, and left a *padrão* (cross) that stands there today to commemorate his stay.

I was eager to press on to Abyssinia where I had heard there were interesting

Portuguese remains. I was not disappointed. The Portuguese were the first Europeans to penetrate this mysterious kingdom in quest of the legendary empire of Prester John. They helped to build the palace of the Emperor Fasilides at Gondar. With its crenellated battlements and elegant brickwork, the castle resembles those of northern Portugal. Apart from the exotic background of its setting it might have come straight from Guimarães or Bragança. Near Gondar there are a number of extremely fine bridges also built by the Portuguese, and a wonderful ruined Baroque church on an island on Lake Tana. Its elegant façade almost overgrown by vegetation, it stands forgotten and unvisited.

From Abyssinia I went first to Aden (the dry, craggy stronghold that Alfonso de Albuquerque failed to capture in 1504: he settled for the nearby island of Socotra instead) and then to Muscat, which remained a Portuguese possession until 1637 and still has two fine Portuguese forts. Then to the island of Ormuz guarding the entrance to the Persian Gulf. I was particularly eager to photograph the remains of the fortress which Albuquerque ordered to be built there when he captured the island in 1507. It has very seldom been photographed and even though I had permission to do so from the Iranian authorities, I was still arrested when I arrived and threatened with the confiscation of my cameras and film. After a great deal of negotiating and checking of credentials, I was allowed to proceed, watched carefully by a police escort. I am glad I got my pictures. Ormuz is a pale shadow of what it once was, but Albuquerque's fortress, though largely in ruins and encroached on by the sea, is one of the great fortifications built by Europeans in the East. It still has its large central keep and a fascinating series of vaulted water cisterns not unlike those found at Mazagan in Morocco. The town it overlooks is a far cry from the one that Milton used in *Paradise Lost* as an ultimate in opulence, when he wrote

> *... the wealth of Ormus and of Ind*
> *Or where the gorgeous East with richest hand*
> *Showers on her kings barbaric pearl and gold.*

The island is a desolate, hot, dusty place today, its landscape enlivened only by the pink and purple of its hills and the distant panorama of gleaming white salt peaks that give it an engaging air of fantasy.

The rest of my trip was spent in India, especially in Goa. Even allowing for the golden glow of retrospect, there is a special quality about Goa, once the Rome of the East, a wealthy emporium of two worlds, and the linchpin holding together Portugal's scattered empire in Asia. Today 'Golden Goa' is no more, the site covered by thick undergrowth. Groves of coconut palms now line the avenues once graced by the houses and gardens of Portuguese *'fidalgos'*. Only a few churches stand witness to the city's splendid past. Of these the seventeenth century Cathedral and the rose-pink church of Bom Jesus, where St. Francis Xavier lies buried, are among the finest architectural treasures left by a European nation in the East.

There is talk of restoring Old Goa, which has become a great tourist attraction as well as a place of pilgrimage for many of Asia's Christians. It would be a pity if it was over-restored or tidied up too much. It is so imbued with the spirit of place and the 'pleasure of ruins' that it would be sad to see it tidied up and labelled. I suspect it is probably far more beautiful as a ruin than it ever was in its undoubtedly gaudy heyday. It belongs to the world of Piranesi, not Disney, and I hope it remains that way.

Portugal left its mark in many other parts of Goa, in some lovely old town and country houses, in a wealth of Indo-Portuguese decorative arts and in the large parish churches which feature in even the smallest villages. Some appear as miniature St. Peter's set down in an exotic tropical setting, huge barn-like structures with few parishioners and only an occasional priest to take services. However, they often come to life on saints' feast days. I remember going to one at the small fishing village of Colva where every year there is a festival of the Infant Jesus, a very popular local event. Fairs, bands, processions, the lot. I was reminded of the numerous accounts of travellers to Goa in its heyday. They comment on the opulence and display that the Portuguese loved to affect. They talk of palanquins and processions, pageants and religious festivals, which were made the excuse for good food, dances and masques. The contrast between the often ostentatious display of finery out-of-doors and the maintenance of almost native simplicity within was a trait noticed by many visitors.

Goa was the largest and wealthiest of the Portuguese settlements in India. But there were others, notably Diu and Damão in the north, tiny enclaves, walled and fortified like mediaeval cities and with a number of beautiful churches. Diu, with its huge fortress jutting out into the sea, is particularly impressive and is almost completeley encircled by the original city walls, with a single narrow main point of entry, not unlike Obidos in Portugal.

Bassein, north of Bombay is another completely walled settlement. It hasn't been a Portuguese possession since the middle of the eighteenth century but it remains an outstanding example, though in ruins, of a mediaeval European city transplanted to the Indian subcontinent.

Other Portuguese forts and settlements on the west coast of India are fascinating, especially at Cranganore, Canonore and Chaul in the south and of course at Cochin and Calicut, where Vasco da Gama landed after his long voyage from Portugal. The exact spot is just north of the town. It is a lovely long, quiet beach fringed by palm trees and very popular with the local fishermen. A simple monument marks the spot where da Gama first set foot on Indian soil. It was here that I finished my own voyage in his wake.

Several years later, thanks to a grant from the Gulbenkian Foundation, I returned to India to continue my photographic coverage of the east coast, especially Madras, and to visit Sri Lanka to see the Portuguese fortress at Galle. From there I went on to Thailand where the Portuguese once had a trading post and mission (at present being excavated) in the old capital of Ayutthaya.

I also visited Malacca. Captured by Albuquerque in 1511, the city remained a Portuguese possession for over a century before being taken by the Dutch. It retains a charming atmosphere with several ruined churches and the remains of the main arch to Albuquerque's fortress 'A Famosa'. It also has a thriving Luso-Malaysian community, who speak a Portuguese dialect of their own called *papiar cristang*.

I wish I had seen some of the Portuguese remains in Indonesia but they are widely scattered and difficult of access. However, I did spend some time on the island of Timor, a place of unforgettable beauty. Few old Portuguese buildings remain there but, in those days at any rate, it still possessed, especially in its remoter corners, a wonderful, undiluted atmosphere of the South Pacific world of Captain Cook.

Macau, my next stop, proved fascinating in many ways; but I expected a greater mixture of styles in its architecture. I found Portuguese and Chinese elements in interesting juxtaposition but without the excitement of suggestive integration I had anticipated. The one exception was the huge façade of the ruined Jesuit church of São Paulo, which was largely built by exiled Japanese Christians in the seventeenth century. This magnificent ruin, a cross between a folly and a monument, stands at the head of a wide, flowing flight of shallow steps, creating a theatrical effect which could never have been achieved if there had been a church behind that elegant, empty façade with its intricate and fascinating mixture of European and Asian elements. I believe that only the Portuguese could have brought them together in such a startling way.

Japan, my last stop, yielded a wealth of interesting examples of *namban* art (i.e. 'southern barbarian', the name the Japanese gave to the Portuguese), especially the screens which depicted with humour and artistic ingenuity the arrival in the sixteenth century of the Portuguese in all their commercial and ecclesiastical splendour.

I spent some time in Nagasaki, the focal point of the so-called Christian Century in Japan, and although nothing tangible remains from the Portuguese period there, one can still stand on the site of the old Jesuit mission of Todos-os-Santos and gaze across to the harbour where the Great Ship from Amacon (Macau) used to sail in on its annual trading mission centuries ago.

When I look back over the record of these journeys and the pictures I took, I can see that in some respects they create a sketchy perspective. Much is omitted, much remains to be done. It is in fact an endless quest, which challenges me as much today as it did when I started out on my travels over thirty years ago. As the years go by I can fit more of the pieces of the jigsaw together. In this respect the Portuguese world, as expressed in its architectural and decorative styles, is an endlessly fascinating study.

The Portuguese have always shown a remarkable ability to accommodate even the most exotic of foreign elements with their own. They were the first to introduce the Orient to Europe. Yet they remain distinctly Portuguese. Conformity alternates (and blends) with great bursts of originality. They are great improvisers and adapters, *pasticheurs*. It is a pattern of contrasts and contradictions, a mixing process, an originality verging on the eccentric, which fascinates me, and when one can trace and follow its distinctive style, flavour and pattern around the world in a multitude of different settings, as I have attempted to do, it becomes a kind of Odyssey.

I hope that the photographs in this book, distilled and edited from the thousands I took on my travels, will tell something of the story of a heritage. Inevitably they reflect a very personal, subjective view but they may have a wider, more general appeal. When I exhibited these pictures in New York, an old lady said to me: 'I know nothing about Portugal and nothing about photography, but I can see that these pictures have been taken with a lot of love.'

Michael. W. Teague

The author by Diogo Cão's inscription
at the Yelala Rapids, River Congo.

The formidable defences the Portuguese constructed
around the Moroccan city of Ceuta,
which they captured from the Moors in 1415.

Arzila was another important early Portuguese
settlement in Morocco.

The early Portuguese navigators hoped that the great rivers
of West Africa would lead them to fabulous wealth
in the interior. A view of the Senegal River
as it flows into the sea at St. Louis.

The 16th century fort at Cacheu in Guiné-Bissau.

The old municipal post still stands in what was once
the main square of the city of Ribeira Grande
(Cidade Velha), the first capital of the Cape Verde Islands.

The ruins of the 16th century cathedral at Ribeira Grande,
Cape Verde.

Cape Verdan silhouette.

The great castle of São Jorge da Mina (Elmina)
was built by the Portuguese in 1482
and remained their most important West African trading post
until it was taken by the Dutch in 1637.

The central courtyard of the castle.

The islands of São Tomé and Principe
in the Gulf of Guinea were discovered by the Portuguese
over five centuries ago.
They retain many attractive vestiges of the past.

There is a spectacular beauty about the two islands.

The self-contained world of the roças (cocoa plantations)
on São Tomé.

Diogo Cão, who discovered the mouth of the River Congo
in 1482, managed to journey some way upstream
before his caravels were turned back at the rapids of Yelala.
On rocks above these rapids
he and his men carved an interesting inscription which,
with the aid of chalk, can still be read today.

Luanda, the capital of Angola,
was founded by the Portuguese in 1575.
It still has many fine examples
of historical architecture,
including this 17th century church of N. S. da Nazaré.

After almost a century of exploratory voyages down the
west coast of Africa, Portuguese navigators
finally reached the southern tip of the continent
and in 1488 Bartolomeu Dias
rounded the Cape of Good Hope.

Dias passed the great Cape of São Brás
(know as Cape St. Blaize today) near Mossel Bay.

At Mossel Bay Dias reprovisioned his ships.
Later navigators, including Vasco da Gama, did the same.

Mozambique Island on the East African coast
soon became an important stopover for Portuguese ships
en route to and from the East.
The narrow streets of the island.

A fine example of 18th century Portuguese architecture
on Mozambique Island.

Mozambique Island retains an attractive atmosphere
of the past.

The 16th century chapel of N. S. do Baluarte on
Mozambique Island is the only existing example of
Manueline art in Africa.

The Portuguese went far up the Zambezi River
in quest of the legendary empire of Monomatapa
and in the 17th century
they founded settlements at Tete and Sena.
Evening on the river near Tete.

The island of Zanzibar was an important Portuguese
trading post for many years.

Fort Jesus in Mombasa (Kenya)
was built by the Portuguese in the 16th century
to protect their interests in East Africa.

The old port of Mombasa.

At Malindi, just north of Mombasa,
Vasco da Gama placed a pillar and cross on a promontory
near the harbour, where they can still be seen today.

One of the original motives
behind Portugal's search for the sea-route to the East
had been the desire to link up
with the empire of Prester John i.e. Abyssinia, (now Ethiopia)
with its curious Christian heritage.

A Coptic monastery near Gondar in Ethiopia.

The Portuguese established themselves at Gondar
(the then capital of Abyssinia)
and helped to build the great castle
of the Emperor Fasilides there.

Interior of the castle at Gondar.

Soon after the discovery of Brazil in 1500,
Salvador da Bahia,
built on the traditional Portuguese pattern
of an upper and a lower town,
became the first capital of this rich new possession.

The churches of Bahia are a great architectural heritage.
N. S. do Pilar dates from the late 18th century.

The church of São Francisco de Assis is one
of the finest in the city.

The ornate, heavily gilded interior of São Francisco.

The early 18th century church
of N. S. da Boa Viagem in Salvador.

The magnificent Baroque church
at Congonhas do Campo in Minas Gerais
is decorated with life-size figures of the Prophets
sculpted by António Francisco Lisboa (O Aleijadinho).

'O Aleijadinho' also designed and decorated
the church of São Francisco de Assis in São João Del-Rei, Minas Gerais.

The original beauty of Rio de Janeiro.

The Largo do Boticário
is one of the oldest corners of the city.

The entrance to the church of Santo Alexandre in Belém
(Pará) which was built by the Jesuits in 1653.

INDIA

The island of Ormuz, guarding the entrance to the Persian
Gulf, was once a great trade emporium.
Captured by Alfonso de Albuquerque in 1507
it remained an important Portuguese possession until 1622.
The ruins of the huge fortress
they built there can still be seen today.

A view of the small town of Ormuz seen from
the fortress ramparts.

Shrine dedicated to St. Francis Xavier in Goa.

Fortresses and churches, the pattern of Old Goa.

A ruined arch
is all that remains of the old Jesuit College in Goa,
which once gave instruction
to over three thousand pupils.

Old tombstones
in the cloister of a forgotten church in Goa.

The church of Bom Jesus
in Goa where St. Francis Xavier lies buried.

The intricately worked coffin in the church contains
the remains of the saint.

The magnificent Manueline entrance to the Church
of São Francisco in Goa.

Interior of the church.

The huge 17th century cathedral in Old Goa.

The parish church at Calengute in Goa.

Indo-Portuguese art shows an interesting mixture of styles.

Indo-Portuguese religious figure.

The ruined churches of Old Goa silhouetted against the
evening sky.

The fortress of Diu at sunset.

Saints' relics, church of Bom Jesus, Goa.

Boats wait for the tide
at the mouth of the River Mandovi in Goa
just as ships from Portugal used to do in olden times.

The entrance to the fortress of Diu in India,
which was started by Alfonso de Albuquerque
early in the 16th century.

The ornate façade of the Jesuit College in Diu.

The entrance to the early 17th century fort
of São Jerónimo, Damão, India.

By the lotus lakes of Damão.

A ruined 16th century church at Bassein, once an
important Portuguese settlement just north of Bombay.

A religious procession enters the Manueline-style entrance
to a church in Cochin.

Pepper was one of the things which brought
the Portuguese to the East.
Sifting a pepper crop at Cochin,
which was once the centre of Portuguese trading activities
along the Malabar Coast in India.

The palm-fringed beach at Calicut where Vasco da Gama
landed in southern India in 1498.

The fortress at Galle in Sri Lanka, which was built by the
Portuguese in the 17th century.

The ruins of the old city of Ayutthaya,
once the capital of Thailand,
where the Portuguese maintained
a church and a trading post in the 17th century.

The canals of Malacca have changed little since the time
the Portuguese established a settlement there in 1511.

Ships still moor near the 'godowns' (warehouses)
at Malacca as they did in olden times.

Only the main portico remains of Albuquerque's fortress
'A Famosa' in Malacca.

The ruins of the church of São Paulo, Malacca,
where the body of St. Francis Xavier was buried for a time
before being removed to Goa.

Traditional houses on the island of Timor.

Timorese chiefs on parade.

Junks at anchor off Macau, which was founded by the
Portuguese in 1557.

A window in Macau.

An interesting juxtaposition of architectural styles in Macau.

Old houses in Macau.

Street scene, Macau.

Façade of the Jesuit church of São Paulo, Macau,
which was built in the 17th century.

The façade seen from the rear.
The church burned down in 1835.

Detail of the façade. The church was built
with the aid of Japanese Christians exiled from their country
in the 17th century.

The inner courtyard of the Leal Senado in Macau.

Street scene, Macau.

Japanese Christians at Mass in Nagasaki.

View of the city of Nagasaki from the site of the church
which the Jesuits built there in the 16th century.

'And if there had been more of the world,
they would have reached it.'
Camões, The Lusiads, VII, 14.